This Book Belongs To:

The Morbid Alphabet Book

Story & Design by:
Gabrielle Ferrara

Illustrations by:
Penji.co

Uniquely Morbid
INVOKING CURIOSITY

Story & Design by Gabrielle Ferrara
Illustrations by Penji.co

Hardcover ISBN: 979-8-9860791-3-4
Paperback ISBN: 979-8-9860791-4-1
EBook ISBN: 979-8-9860791-5-8

Library of Congress Control Number: 2022910928

www.UniquelyMorbid.com

This one is for you Mom! Thanks for always encouraging me to follow my dreams. Love you!

A is for...

Apothecary

- the pharmacist of old.

Apothecary

(Uh·paa·thuh·keh·ree)

A person who prepares and sells medicinal treatments for a variety of ailments. Apothecary is a historical term and profession similar to a modern pharmacist. Some apothecaries even trained as surgeons!

B is for...

Bones

- all 206 of them.

Bones

(Bownz)

A living tissue that provides structural support for vertebrate animals. Human infants are born with 300 bones, mainly composed of cartilage. As the infant grows, some bones will fuse, leaving the adult human with only 206 bones. More than half of those 206 bones are in the hands and feet.

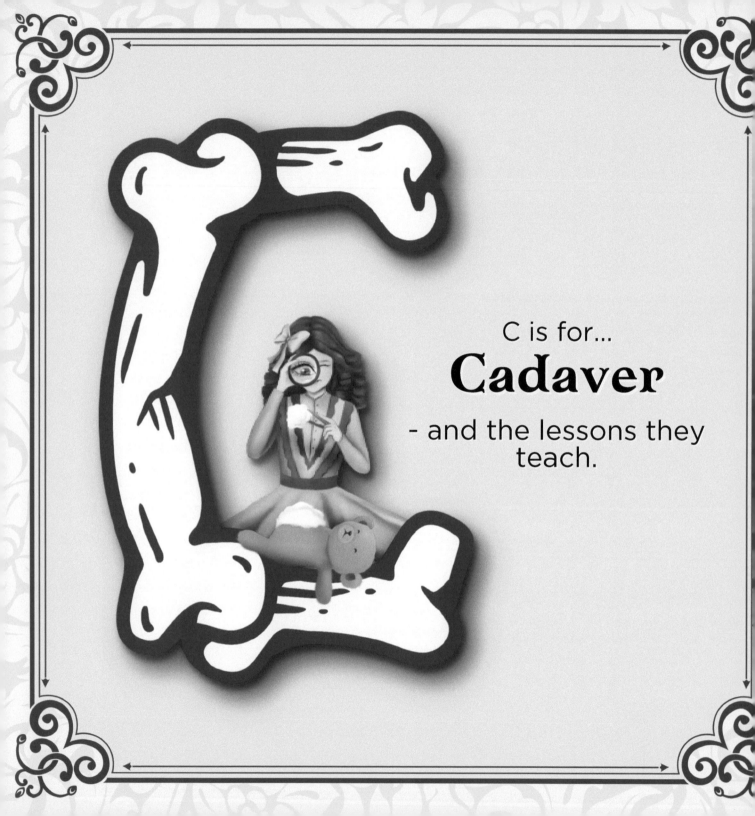

C is for...
Cadaver

- and the lessons they teach.

Cadaver

(Cah·dah·ver)

A human corpse donated for scientific research. Medical professionals, anthropologists, and scientists use cadavers to learn more about human bodies. A medical examiner carefully dissects and studies cadavers to detect any signs of disease, cause of death, medical anomalies, internal structures, etc.

D is for...
Death
- the collector of souls.

Death

(Deth)

The end of life. Death is the final stage in the life cycle of humans and animals. Cultures throughout history have depicted and described death with human-like characteristics. Applying human traits to abstract ideas is called personification. One of the most popular personifications of death is the Grim Reaper.

E is for...

Exsanguinate

- a horrible mess
to clean.

Exsanguinate

(Ick·sang·gwuh·nate)

The removal of mass quantities of blood from the body. Exsanguination typically occurs while the animal or human is still alive, but it can also happen after death. Embalmers prepare deceased bodies for funerals by draining the blood from the body and replacing it with embalming fluid.

F is for...
Fungus
- thriving on decay.

Fungus

(Fun·gus)

A spore-producing organism that feeds on organic material. Some examples of fungus include mold, mushrooms, and yeast. Cordyceps are parasitic fungi that prey on insects and turn them into zombies. As the fungus grows, it will erupt from the insect's body and eventually consume it.

G is for...

Grotesque

- the ugliest sight
you will see.

Grotesque

(Grow·tesk)

A being or object that is absurdly hideous, strange, uncomfortable, distorted, or ugly. During the Medieval period, across Europe, gothic architecture incorporated grotesque statues. These monstrous creatures would scare off evil spirits and protect the building from harm.

H is for...

Haruspicy

- "What could this mean?"

Haruspicy

(Ha·rus·pie·see)

An ancient form of divination that uses the entrails of an animal to predict or foretell omens. Numerous cultures practiced haruspicy throughout history. Haruspicy can be dated back to at least 700 B.C.E. The liver was the most sought-after organ to use.

I is for...
Infection
- "Scrub a dub dub."

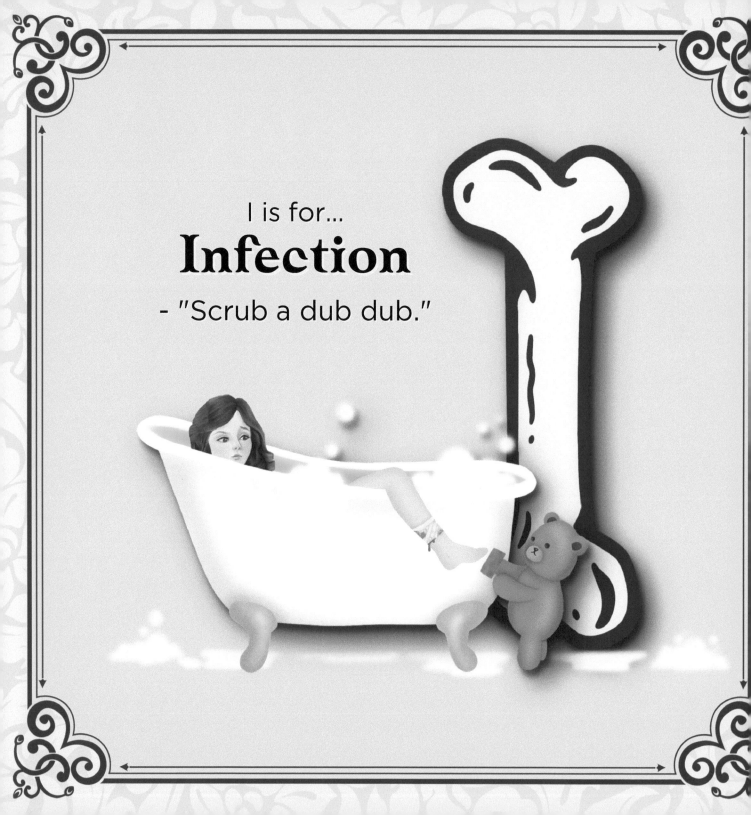

Infection

(In·feck·shun)

A disease caused by the invasion of germs in one or more of the body tissues. Germs such as bacteria, viruses, prions, and fungi are microorganisms. An infection left untreated can spread to other parts of the body and eventually lead to death. Doctors recommend practicing good hygiene to prevent this.

J is for...

Janiform

- two heads are better
than one.

Janiform

(Jan·ee·form)

Resembling the Roman god Janus by having two faces. A similar word to "janiform" is "bicephaly". Bicephaly is a genetic condition that results in an animal being born with two heads. Two-headed animals were a common attraction at sideshow events.

K is for...
Knell
- music for the departed.

Knell

(Nell)

The sound produced by solemnly rung bells. This sound is most often associated with funerals. Another name for "Knell" is "Death Knell". Historically, church bells were rung at three separate times related to a person's death: before, during, and after.

L is for...
Larvae
- the hungry little grubs.

Larvae

(Lar·vah)

The infant stage of the life cycle for invertebrate animals with indirect development into adulthood. "Larvae" is the plural form of "larva". At the larva stage, the animal will not resemble its adult form. Many Amphibians and insects have a larva stage. "Maggot" is the larva stage of any insect that feasts on decaying materials.

M is for...
Macabre

- and morbid curiosity.

Macabre

(Mah·cob)

Related to death or the horrors of death. Macabre can also mean gruesome, ghastly, or disturbing. Postmortem photography is an example of a Victorian-era tradition that many people today would find macabre. In postmortem photography, the deceased person is staged to look as if they are still alive. Children were the most common subject of postmortem photography. This tradition was a form of mourning, and often it was the only picture of the deceased family member.

N is for...

Necropsy

– solving animal crimes.

Necropsy

(Neh·crop·see)

The medical examination of an animal's body after death to determine how the animal died. The word "necropsy" is similar to and often mistaken for "autopsy". An autopsy only occurs when a human conducts a postmortem medical examination on another human. Necropsy, however, can refer to the postmortem examination of any animal performed by any species.

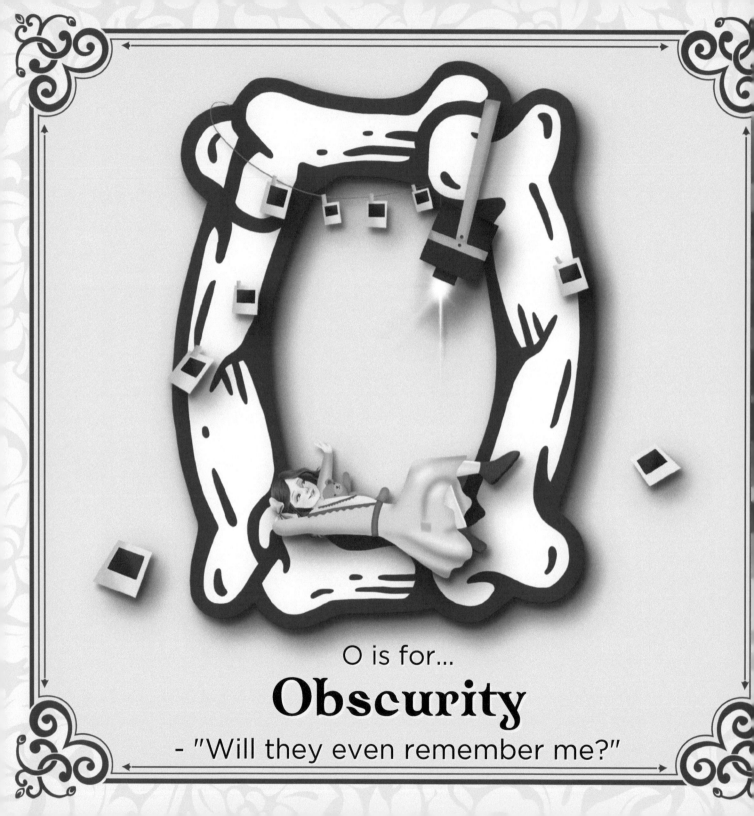

O is for...

Obscurity

- "Will they even remember me?"

Obscurity

(Ob·scur·uh·tee)

Unknown, unclear, forgotten, or difficult to understand. When a person fades into obscurity, they become difficult to recognize.

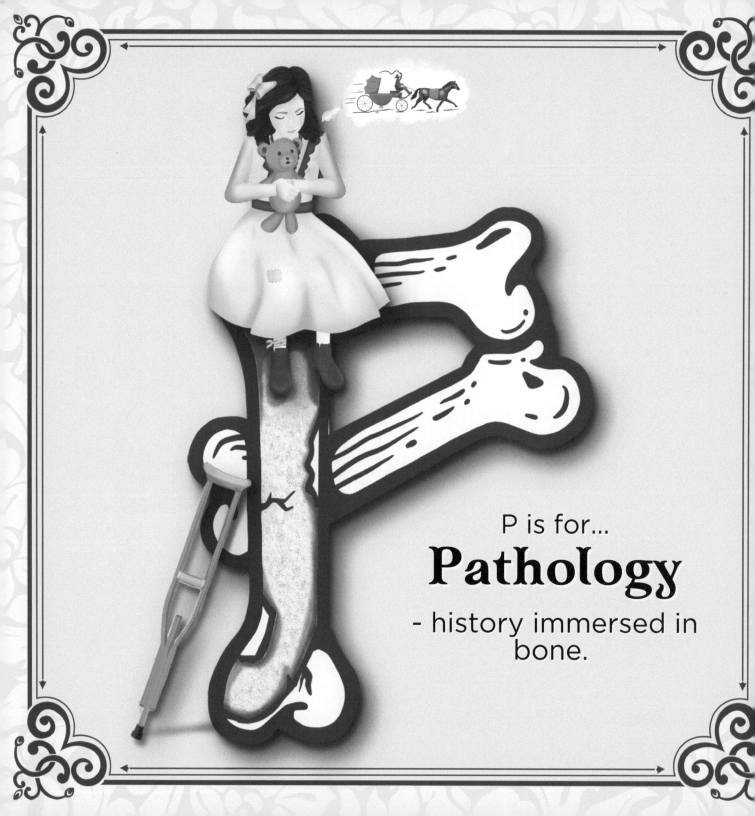

P is for...
Pathology
- history immersed in bone.

Pathology

(Path·ol·oh·gee)

The scientific study of disease and injury. Bone is a living tissue that will respond to disease and injury by regrowing and healing itself. Bone regrowth is remarkably different in texture than healthy bone, making pathology relatively easy to spot.

Q is for...

Quietus

- an acquaintance
of death.

Quietus

(Qui·ee·tus)

The release from life. Similar to the word "death", quietus signifies the ending. Quietus can also refer to a calm and quiet atmosphere where all activity has stopped.

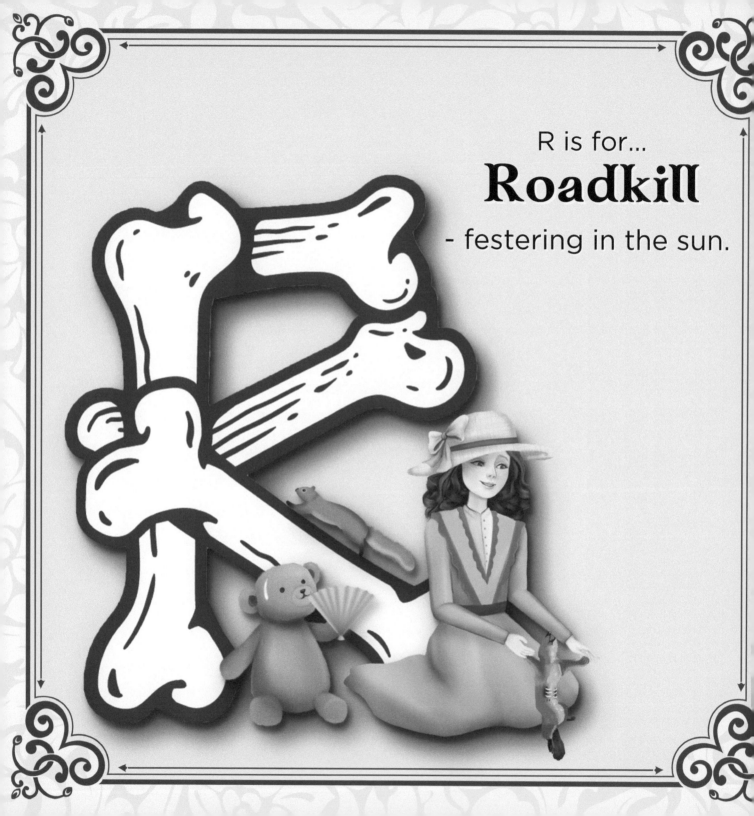

R is for...
Roadkill

- festering in the sun.

Roadkill

(Rowd·kil)

The remains of an animal left on the ground after being killed by a vehicle in motion. Over 40 million squirrels a year become roadkill. Scientists can use roadkill to track invasive species and population growth.

S is for...
Skeleton
- nothing left to spoil.

Skeleton

(Skel·uh·ton)

A structural framework that supports an animal's body. There are three types of skeletons: endoskeleton, exoskeleton, and hydrostatic. Endoskeletons are internal and usually composed of bone. An exoskeleton is an external hard casing. Hydrostatic skeletons are formed by fluid-filled compartments.

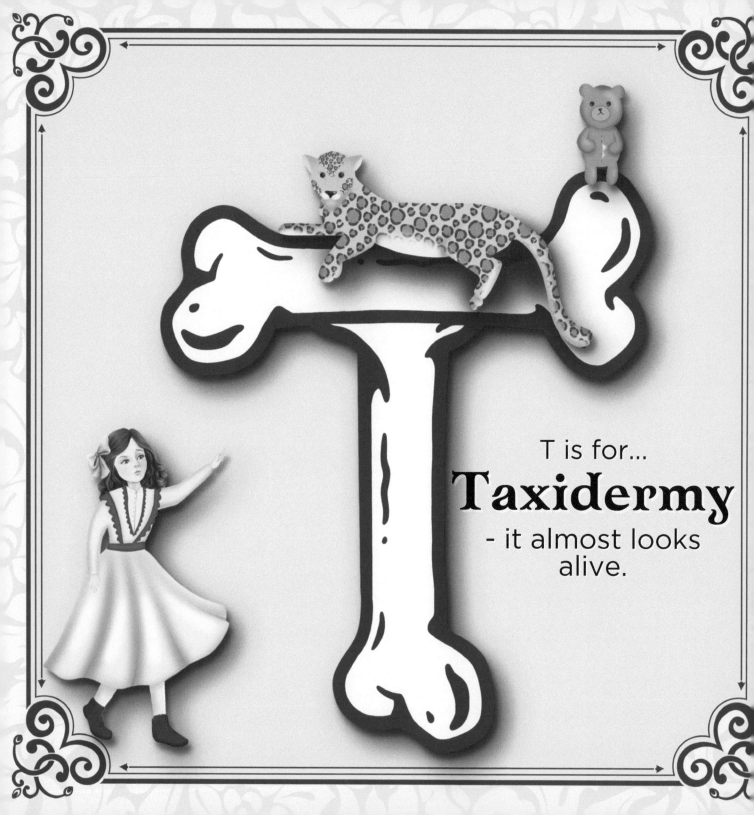

T is for...
Taxidermy
- it almost looks alive.

Taxidermy

(Tax·uh·dur·me)

The art of preserving a dead animal with a lifelike appearance by stuffing and mounting its skin. During the Victorian era, one of the most popular forms of taxidermy were anthropomorphic scenes. In an anthropomorphic scene, animals and non-human objects have human qualities and characteristics.

U is for...
Undead

- "Mmmmm, brains."

Undead

(uhn·ded)

Something which is dead but continues to behave as if it were still alive. Famous examples of the undead include vampires and zombies.

V is for...
Vomitous

- the sweet smell of decay.

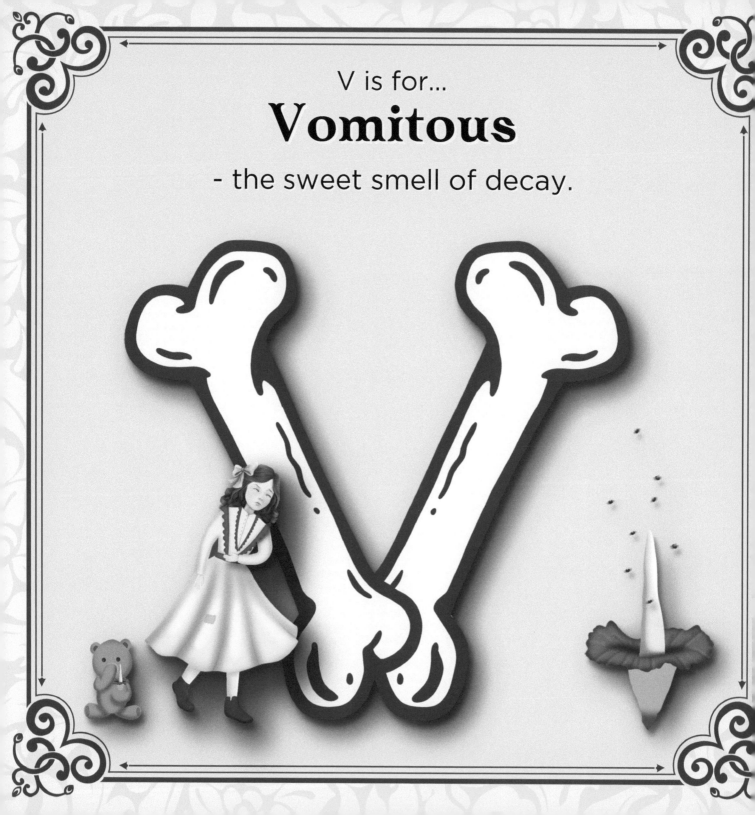

Vomitous

(Vom·uht·iss)

An object that causes someone to feel nauseous, sick, or disgusted. The corpse flower (amorphophallus titanum) is aptly named for the putrid odor it releases as it blooms—about once every ten years. The blooming event can last up to 36 hours before the flowers collapse.

W is for...

Wraith

- a haunting like no other.

Wraith

(Ray·th)

An apparition of someone shortly before or after they die. The wraith's appearance is eerily similar to the person who either has or soon will be deceased. However, apparitions that occur months or even years after a person has died are not wraiths; they belong to a different category of ghosts.

X is for...
Xyster
- for the cleanest of bones.

Xyster

(Zis·ter)

A medical tool surgeons use to scrape bone. A xyster removes thin layers of bone, allowing clean tissue to appear. Surgeons from all medical fields, including veterinarians, will use a xyster when necessary.

Y is for...
Yarpha

- where mummies lie
beneath.

Yarpha

(Yar·fa)

Soil composed of peat and sand. Peat is the accumulation of decaying plants and organic materials. Archaeologists across the world have found mummified humans, animals, and skeletal remains inside layers of peat. These discoveries are more commonly known as bog mummies.

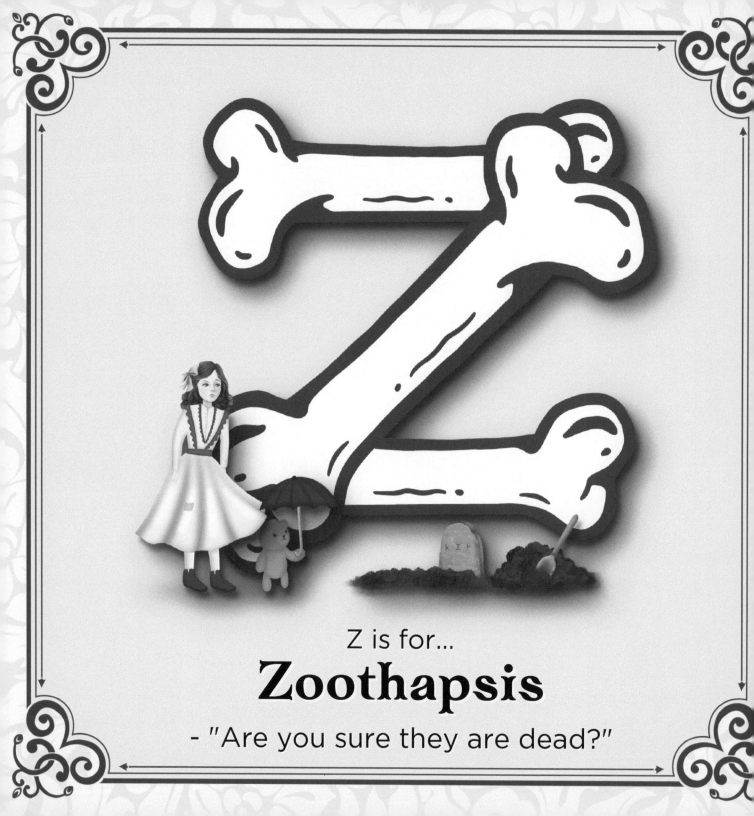

Z is for...
Zoothapsis
- "Are you sure they are dead?"

Zoothapsis

(Zuth·app·sis)

A burial that happened while the person was still alive. Safety coffins were invented as a solution to zoothapsis. These specialty coffins date back to the late 1700s and varied in design. One of the most well-known examples of a safety coffin had a string inside that attached to a bell located above ground. If the human inside the coffin woke up, they would pull on the string and pray for rescue.

Lilian Everly

October 31, 1865 –
November 13, 1874

Gabrielle Ferrara is an artist and entrepreneur who creates Victorian inspired art and jewelry with ethically sourced animal remains. She has a master's degree in Museum Studies and undergraduate degrees in Anthropology and Art History. Gabrielle enjoys spending her free time with family, venturing down the rabbit hole of obscurity, and talking about dinosaurs.

 @UniquelyMorbid
www.UniquelyMorbid.com